Guiding Luna's Light
A Companion for Moms and Mentors

WENDY LEONARD

Copyright © 2025 Wendy Leonard

ISBN: 979-8-9997481-1-9

I0518510

DEDICATION

To the moms, mentors, teachers, aunties, sisters, coaches, and all those who show up for our girls — this book is for you.

For anyone who listens with their whole heart and walks beside her when her heart breaks — thank you for seeing the light in her even if she can't, just yet.

May this guide support you as you help her become a woman who never forgets that she is lovable, beautiful, and has so much to offer this world.

And if you need to be reminded of this yourself, may you also find healing in this journey.

CONTENTS

INTRODUCTION: GUIDING HER LIGHT, HONORING YOUR OWN LIGHT

If you're holding this guide, chances are you're someone who cares deeply about a girl navigating her way through the confusing, beautiful, and often overwhelming tween years. Whether you're a parent, teacher, counselor, aunt, or mentor — this book was created for you.

The Light Inside Luna isn't just a story. It's a doorway. A mirror. A gentle nudge for girls to begin discovering their inner voice, their sense of worth, and their power to choose how they show up in the world. This guide is here to help you walk alongside them.

Why This Guide Exists

Girls today are growing up in a culture saturated with messages that can dim their light before they even know it's there. They are absorbing stories about their worth, their bodies, and their value — some of which they never speak aloud.

This guidebook exists to spark the conversations that often go unsaid. It's designed to help you:

- Create meaningful connections through Luna's story

- Explore important themes like self-worth, friendship, body image, and belonging

- Reflect on your own journey — because, often, the path to guiding her light is remembering how to tend to your own

What to Expect

Inside, you'll find chapter-by-chapter reflections, journal prompts, discussion starters, and small activities you can use to make reading *The Light Inside Luna* a more engaging and healing experience — for both of you.

A Note About Spirituality

Throughout this guide, you'll find references to biblical scripture woven into certain sections. These are included as a source of grounding, wisdom, and hope — but they are not meant to limit your journey or prescribe a single path.

You are welcome to substitute these with words, poems, teachings, or practices from your own faith, tradition, or personal beliefs. What matters most is inviting in a spiritual thread — something greater than ourselves to lean on, especially as our girls grow and begin to realize that they cannot rely on others to fill this space within them.

However you choose to approach it, may this companion encourage you to explore and share the spiritual roots that give you strength, and to help her discover her own.

A Note Before You Begin

You don't need to be perfect to guide a girl through her growing-up years. You just need to be present. Curious. Willing to listen more than you speak. Willing to hold space for her confusion without rushing to fix it.

There's no right or wrong way to use this guide. Read it alongside your daughter or student, or use it to deepen your own understanding before bringing topics up casually — at the dinner table, in the car, or during a quiet moment before bed.

This guide will give you the tools, but you bring the essence — your presence, your example, your light.

Thank you for showing up.
Thank you for helping her see that she is not alone.
And thank you for being part of the quiet revolution of raising girls who know their worth.

Now let's begin.

1 ONE COMMENT

Chapter Summary for Moms & Mentors

In this opening chapter, Luna's world shifts with just a few careless words: *"Wow, your legs are…big."* It's a passing comment — but it lands deep. Up until that moment, Luna had never questioned her body. Suddenly, something innocent becomes something heavy. Her self-awareness sharpens, not with wonder, but with shame.

This is the moment many girls will recognize, even if they've never spoken it aloud: the first time they saw their body as "wrong."

Themes to Explore

- Body image and first wounds

- The power of words

- Shame and self-consciousness

- Early social comparison

- Losing trust in your body

Reflect & Connect

For you, Mama (or Mentor):

1. Do you remember the first time *you* felt self-conscious about your body? What triggered it?

2. What messages did you grow up hearing about body size, food, or appearance?

3. Have you ever made a passing comment (about yourself or someone else) that might have stuck with your daughter?

4. How do you model body respect and self-talk in front of her?

Journal Prompt

Write a note of compassion to your younger self at the moment you began to feel ashamed of your body.

Discussion Starters

These can be casual or done while walking, journaling, or driving — no pressure.

- How do you think Luna felt when someone commented on her legs?

- Why do you think it stuck with her?

- Has anything like that ever happened to you or someone you know?

- What do you think makes our bodies valuable?

Tip: If she's quiet, just listening is enough. Sharing your own experience first can help her feel safe.

Creative Prompt or Activity

Grab a pack of sticky notes. Write down words of truth and affirmation together, like:

- "My legs help me run and jump."

- "God made every part of me on purpose."

- "My body deserves love and care."

Have her stick them on a mirror, notebook, or closet door.
(You do it too. Let her see you honor your own body.)

Scripture Reflection

"I praise You because I am fearfully and wonderfully made; Your works are wonderful, I know that full well." — Psalm 139:14

Ask her:

- What do you think "wonderfully made" means?

- Do you believe it's true about *you*? Why or why not?

Help her explore what God says about her body, not the world.

Closing Words for You

One comment can plant shame.
But one safe conversation — one moment of listening, one spoken truth — can begin to pull it out by the roots.

You are not just protecting her body image.
You're helping her remember the truth of who she is before the world tried to tell her otherwise.

And if you're still healing your own relationship with your body, know this: your journey is sacred too.

You both deserve to live free.

2 WHAT DO SKINNY GIRLS EAT?

Chapter Summary for Moms & Mentors

In this chapter, Luna begins to search for answers to a question that quietly consumes her: *What do skinny girls eat?* What starts as curiosity becomes a deepening spiral into comparison, rules, and restriction—fueled by the curated, filtered world of social media. Luna isn't just looking for food tips — she's looking for belonging, control, and a version of herself that feels worthy.

This chapter exposes a modern truth: many girls are being taught more by TikTok and Instagram than by real-life voices of wisdom and love.

Themes to Explore

- Body comparison and the influence of social media
- The desire for control through food
- Early signs of disordered thinking
- Appearance-based self-worth
- The pressure to shrink to be accepted

Reflect & Connect

For you, Mama (or Mentor):

1. Have you ever googled or followed trends about "what to eat" to change your body? Where did that path lead you?

2. How do you talk about food, weight, and health around your daughter?

3. Are there accounts or influencers your daughter follows that concern you? Have you asked her what shows up on her "For You" page?

4. What were you taught about "good" and "bad" foods growing up?

Journal Prompt

Write down the food rules or body ideals you absorbed growing up. Which ones do you still carry, and which ones are you ready to let go of —for her and for you?

Discussion Starters

These should be handled gently — let her lead and try not to correct, just stay curious.

- Why do you think Luna started asking that question?

- Have you ever wondered something like that — or seen people talk about it online?

- What do you think is the difference between real health and what's just trending?

- How do you feel when you see certain pictures or videos of other girls or influencers?

Tip: If you sense she's uncomfortable, let her know you're not judging. You're just here to listen and walk beside her.

Creative Prompt or Activity

Cut out images or words that represent food for:

- Body (nutrition, strength)

- Mind (learning, curiosity)

- Soul (friendship, prayer, music, nature)

Create a collage titled: *What Nourishes Me.*
Remind her: food isn't just about appearance—it's about energy, joy, connection, and life.

Option: Add affirmations like "My body deserves kindness" or "Food is fuel, not punishment."

Scripture Reflection

"Do not conform to the pattern of this world, but be transformed by the renewing of your mind." — Romans 12:2

Talk about:

- What does "the pattern of this world" look like for girls right now?

- How can we renew our minds — especially when we're overwhelmed by comparison?

You might even talk about practical ways to curate her feed, mute harmful content, and seek truth instead.

Closing Words for You

Your daughter is growing up in a world that profits off her insecurity.

But you — through your love, your language, your faith, and your presence — are one of the strongest voices she'll ever hear.

You don't need to have perfect answers.
You just need to remind her, again and again, that her worth is not something she has to chase, filter, or earn.

You are helping her come home to herself.

3 THE BATTLE IN MY BRAIN

Chapter Summary for Moms & Mentors

In this chapter, Luna starts to notice the war within herself. One part of her wants to be free — eating ice cream, laughing, feeling light. But another voice inside whispers rules, shame, and guilt. Her mind feels like a battlefield of "should" and "should not." The joy she once felt around food and her body is slowly being replaced with anxiety and self-criticism.

This is where many girls begin to split — between who they are and who they think they need to become to be accepted.

Themes to Explore

- Inner conflict and mental noise

- Food guilt and fear-based thinking

- Perfectionism vs. freedom

- Listening to false voices

- Early signs of anxiety or disordered thinking

Reflect & Connect

For you, Mama (or Mentor):

1. Can you recall a time in your life when your thoughts felt like a war zone? What helped you find peace?

2. How do you personally handle guilt, especially around food, parenting, or appearance?

3. What do you model to your daughter about failure, flexibility, and grace?

4. When your daughter talks negatively about herself or her choices, how do you typically respond?

Journal Prompt

Write a letter to the younger version of yourself who was caught in overthinking or self-judgment. What truth does she need to hear?

Discussion Starters

Let these unfold naturally. The goal is not to fix, but to invite her into self-awareness.

- What do you think Luna meant by a "battle in her brain"?

- Do you ever feel like your brain is saying opposite things at the same time?

- If you could draw the two voices Luna hears, what would they look or sound like?

- How do you know which voice to listen to?

Tip: Let her share without rushing to reframe. This is where trust is built.

Creative Prompt or Activity

Invite her to give names or characters to the different voices in her head:

- The one that's critical or harsh (e.g., "The Bully," "The Rule Maker")

- The one that's kind, curious, or wise (e.g., "The Real Me," "Truth Teller")

Then: Have her write a short dialogue between them.
You can do it too. Compare them. Laugh together. Make it light — but insightful.

Option: Draw them or assign them colors. Help her see that *she* gets to decide which voice leads.

Scripture Reflection

"We take captive every thought to make it obedient to Christ." — 2 Corinthians 10:5

This is such a powerful verse when it comes to mental battles.
Ask her:

- What do you think it means to "take a thought captive"?

- Can we choose which thoughts to believe?

- How can God help us know which ones are lies?

Encourage her to pray or journal when her thoughts feel overwhelming. Invite God into the noise.

Closing Words for You

Your daughter is learning how to think — and how to *talk* to herself. You have the beautiful opportunity to help shape that inner dialogue with compassion, truth, and grace.

You can't always quiet the battle in her brain. But you can be her safe place while she learns how to fight with wisdom — not fear.

And as she heals… so do you.

4 THE CRASH

Chapter Summary for Moms & Mentors

In this chapter, Luna feels tired — not just in her body, but in her spirit. The effort of keeping up appearances, overthinking every bite, and comparing herself to others has drained her. Activities she once loved now feel dull. Her laughter doesn't come as easily. This is more than sadness — it's a soul-deep depletion.

What Luna is experiencing is what many girls go through silently: emotional burnout from pretending, performing, and people-pleasing.

Themes to Explore

- Emotional exhaustion and early signs of burnout

- Loss of joy or interest in usual activities

- The mental load of perfectionism and body obsession

- Disconnection from self

- Shame, sadness, and the beginning of withdrawal

Reflect & Connect

For you, Mama (or Mentor):

1. Have you ever reached a point where you felt emotionally or spiritually drained? What led to your "crash"?

2. How do you model rest, joy, and emotional replenishment in your daily life?

3. What signals tell you that your daughter is overwhelmed or emotionally "shut down"?

4. What's your personal relationship with rest? Do you feel permission to slow down — or guilt?

Journal Prompt

What brings you joy that you've put on the back burner? What's one small thing you can return to this week?

Discussion Starters with Your Daughter

Gently open space to explore her emotional world.

- What do you think made Luna feel so depleted?

- Have you ever felt that way — tired even when you're not doing much?

- Is there something you used to love doing that doesn't feel fun anymore?

- What helps you feel like yourself again when you're overwhelmed?

Tip: Normalize rest and sadness. You might say, "It's okay to feel low sometimes. You don't have to earn rest or joy."

Creative Prompt or Activity

Take some time together to reflect on the things that feel draining and the things that feel life-giving. Invite your daughter to think about situations, thoughts, or habits that leave her feeling tired, anxious, or disconnected from herself. Then gently shift the conversation toward the activities, people, or moments that bring her peace, energy, or a sense of joy.

You might say, "Let's each make a list of things that feel heavy — and things that help us feel more like ourselves."

After reflecting, encourage her to choose one item from her joy-filled list that she can return to this week. It could be something small — like painting, walking outside, listening to music, journaling, or playing with a pet. The goal is not productivity, but replenishment.

If you'd like, write each joyful activity on a strip of paper and place them in a small jar together. Call it your *Joy Jar* — a place she can return to when she's feeling low, unsure, or just needs a reminder of what brings her back to life.

This simple exercise reminds her (and you) that joy doesn't need to be earned. It's part of her design — and she's allowed to choose it.

Scripture Reflection

"Come to me, all you who are weary and burdened, and I will give you rest." — Matthew 11:28

Ask her:

- What do you think Jesus means by "rest"?

- Do you think God cares when we feel tired or sad?

- What does it mean to rest on the *inside*?

Encourage her to imagine rest not just as sleeping — but as returning to who she truly is.

Closing Words for You

When your daughter feels depleted, your first instinct may be to fix it — but what she likely needs most is your quiet presence and your permission to rest.

Remind her that joy isn't something she has to earn.
That even Jesus rested.
That being human means having limits — and honoring them is not weakness, it's wisdom.

And as you help her find her joy again… maybe you'll rediscover pieces of your own.

5 SOMEONE WHO SEES ME

Chapter Summary for Moms & Mentors

In this chapter, Luna finally begins to exhale. After carrying around the shame of that comment at school and the quiet spiral that followed, someone finally names what she's been feeling. Tessa's mom, with gentle strength and clear love, opens up a conversation that Luna didn't even know she needed.

She tells Luna the truth: *Your body is not a problem to fix.* It's a part of you that deserves kindness. That moment lands like sunlight after a long winter.

So many girls are desperate for someone — *anyone*, to interrupt the noise and speak this kind of truth.

Themes to Explore

- The healing power of being seen and heard
- Truth-telling from a trusted adult
- Body respect vs. body shame
- Healthy adult modeling
- Kindness toward self as a healing practice

Reflect & Connect

For you, Mama (or Mentor):

1. Has someone ever said something kind to you about your body or your worth that truly changed how you saw yourself?

2. Have you ever *been* that voice for someone else? What helped you step into that role with compassion?

3. What kind of messages do you hope your daughter is hearing about her body from other adults?

4. What holds you back from saying those things out loud to her—
   or to yourself?

Journal Prompt

Write a short note to your daughter (or any girl you love) that begins:
Your body is not a problem... Let the words flow from your heart, not your
head.

Discussion Starters

Let this be a heart-softening chapter. Trust builds here.

- How do you think Luna felt when Tessa's mom spoke up?

- What did you think of the idea that "our bodies are not
  problems to fix"?

- Do you think your body deserves kindness? Why or why not?

- If someone else you cared about was being hard on their body,
  what would you want them to know?

Tip: If she struggles to answer, don't press. Sometimes just sitting with
these questions together is powerful enough.

Creative Prompt or Activity

Invite your daughter to choose one part of her body that she has
struggled with or felt unsure about — maybe her legs, her belly, her
hair, her nose.

Then, ask her to write a short note or letter to that body part, not from
a place of judgment, but from compassion. She can begin with:

"Dear _____, I've been hard on you. I've said things I didn't mean.
But the truth is..."

Encourage her to thank that part of her body for what it does — not
how it looks. For example:
"My legs carry me."

"My belly holds my laughter."

"My arms help me hug my favorite people."

You can write a note to your own body too. Let her see that this is a lifelong practice — not something girls outgrow.

Scripture Reflection

"The Lord does not look at the things people look at. People look at the outward appearance, but the Lord looks at the heart." — 1 Samuel 16:7

Talk about:

- What do *we* tend to focus on when we look at people?

- What do you think God sees when He looks at you?

Let her sit in the truth that her body is not her value. And neither is yours.

Closing Words for You

This is the kind of chapter that can change a girl's story.

When a trusted adult tells the truth with gentleness — that her body is not something to fix, that her worth is already intact — it plants a seed that shame cannot uproot.

Be that voice, again and again. Not only with words, but with the way you honor your own body, speak truth in front of her, and offer your presence without pressure.

Your seeing her — really seeing her — is part of her healing.

6 MORE THAN ENOUGH

Chapter Summary for Moms & Mentors

In this chapter, Luna is welcomed into a home where food is joy, not judgment. Where mealtimes are filled with laughter, warmth, and flavor — not rules and restriction. At Sandy's house, Luna sees a family that honors tradition and welcomes abundance.

But the most powerful moment comes when Sandy's older sister, Sonja, brings Luna to a special family mirror — a treasured heirloom passed down through generations. She gently asks Luna to really *see* herself. Not to analyze, shrink, or hide—but to stand tall and witness the beauty that has always been there. In Sonja's culture, curves are honored. Fullness is celebrated. Luna's body is not just accepted — it's admired.

This chapter is an invitation — for Luna, and for all of us — to reimagine beauty through the lens of love and legacy.

Themes to Explore

- Food as celebration and connection
- Cultural wisdom and reverence for curves
- Seeing your body through a lens of love
- Beauty as generational, soulful, and diverse
- Receiving affirmation from other women

Reflect & Connect

For you, Mama (or Mentor):

1. What messages did your family or culture send about food growing up? Was food joyful, controlled, or complicated?

2. How do you talk about food in your home today? Do meals feel restrictive, rushed, or celebratory?

3. Have you ever had a moment — like Luna's with the mirror — where you saw yourself through someone else's loving eyes?

4. How often do you speak beauty over your daughter that goes beyond appearance — into her presence, spirit, or strength?

Journal Prompt

Describe a moment in your life when food felt sacred or joyful. What do you want to pass on to the next generation about food and body?

Discussion Starters

Let this be an uplifting conversation — infused with warmth and delight.

- What did Luna notice about how Sandy's family treats food and meals?

- How did Sonja help Luna see herself differently?

- Have you ever had someone speak something kind about your appearance or spirit that really stayed with you?

- What does it mean to you to be "more than enough"?

Tip: This chapter is a great chance to reflect together on culture, family, and beauty as something inherited, not manufactured.

Creative Prompt or Activity

Inspired by the moment with Sonja, invite your daughter to stand in front of a mirror — not to inspect, but to *see*. You can do it too.

Have her gently place one hand over her heart and say aloud:

- "This is my body. It is not a problem. It is a gift."

- "My shape is part of my story."

- "I am more than enough."

You might also invite her to write an *Affirmation of Being Enough* and tape it to the mirror:

"I am not here to shrink. I am here to shine."

Make this a ritual — a reclaiming. Not a one-time moment, but something to return to as needed.

Scripture Reflection

"You are altogether beautiful, my darling; there is no flaw in you." — Song of Solomon 4:7

Talk about:

- What does it mean that God sees us as "altogether beautiful"?

- Can beauty be about more than looks? What else makes someone beautiful?

- How does it feel to know that you are fully seen and still fully loved?

Encourage her to write this verse somewhere she'll see it often.

Closing Words for You

This chapter reminds us that girls need more than permission to exist in their bodies — they need celebration. They need examples of joy around food, reverence for curves, and mirrors that reflect truth, not shame.

Let your home be that mirror. Let your language around meals and bodies be filled with grace and delight. Let your legacy be one of love, not lack.

Because your daughter is already more than enough.
And maybe… you are too.

7 LITTLE BY LITTLE

Chapter Summary for Moms & Mentors

In this chapter, something subtle but powerful is happening inside Luna. She's beginning to think differently, feel differently, *see* differently. The harsh voice in her mind is a little quieter. The joy around food is starting to return. And most importantly, she's beginning to look at herself with a bit more softness, a bit more grace.

It's not dramatic or loud — but it's real.
Healing isn't a straight line. It often looks like this: small moments of choosing love over fear, truth over lies, nourishment over control.

And that's what Luna is doing.
Little by little.

Themes to Explore

- Healing as a gradual process

- Progress over perfection

- Rebuilding trust with food

- Self-compassion and inner safety

- Learning to quiet the inner critic

Reflect & Connect

For you, Mama (or Mentor):

1. Have you ever experienced a slow shift in how you saw yourself or your body — one that took time but truly changed you?

2. Do you give yourself permission to grow *little by little*, or do you expect instant change?

3. How do you respond when your daughter makes progress — but then has a hard day or takes a step back?

4. What do you model about resilience, flexibility, and being kind to yourself in the process?

Journal Prompt

Write down three "little by little" ways you've grown — mentally, emotionally, or spiritually. What helped you keep going?

Discussion Starters

This chapter is a great one to affirm her process, not just outcomes.

- What do you think is shifting for Luna in this chapter?

- Has there ever been a time when something got easier — not all at once, but slowly?

- What's one thing about yourself that you're learning to love, even just a little bit?

- When the inner critic shows up, what helps you speak to yourself more kindly?

Tip: Celebrate any moment of vulnerability or self-reflection she offers. This is the kind of chapter that builds trust and hope.

Creative Prompt or Activity

Invite your daughter to start a *"Little by Little Jar"*. Each day (or once a week), she can write one small moment where she noticed herself:

- Thinking a kind thought

- Enjoying food without guilt

- Speaking truth to herself

- Choosing rest or joy

Write it on a small slip of paper and place it in a jar. Over time, she'll have a collection of quiet wins to remind her of her growth.

You can do it too — model it by adding your own slips and sharing them together.

Scripture Reflection

"And I am certain that God, who began the good work within you, will continue His work until it is finally finished." — Philippians 1:6

Talk about:

- What does it mean that God is *still working* in us?

- How can we trust that even small steps matter?

- What's something you want God to keep helping you grow in?

This verse is a beautiful anchor for any girl who feels like she has to "arrive" all at once. Let her know: progress is sacred. Tiny steps count.

Closing Words for You

You don't need to rush her transformation.
You just need to walk beside her as she slowly sheds shame, invites kindness, and remembers the truth of who she is.

Little by little, she's healing.
Little by little, she's learning to love herself.
And little by little — you might be too.

Don't miss the miracle of slow, steady growth.
This is the heart of the work.

8 MY REAL HEALTH PROJECT

Chapter Summary for Moms & Mentors

In this chapter, Luna begins working on her school wellness project. At first, she considers writing something generic — what she thinks teachers want to hear. But then something shifts. She decides to be real.

No more hiding behind food pyramids or fake smiles.
No more pretending she hasn't struggled.

As she sits with her thoughts, Luna begins to tell the truth — to herself first:
That she stopped trusting her body.
That she felt alone and ashamed.
That she tried to fix something that was never broken.

And then... she begins to redefine what *real health* means.
Not just salads or workouts or numbers.
But kindness. Connection. Joy. Curiosity. Wholeness.

This is the moment Luna begins reclaiming her story — not to impress anyone, but to be honest with herself. That's where healing becomes real.

Themes to Explore

- Redefining health through honesty

- Self-reflection and emotional growth

- Moving from shame to self-awareness

- Owning your story, quietly and powerfully

- Letting go of perfection

Reflect & Connect

For you, Mama (or Mentor):

1. If you had been given a "health project" at Luna's age, what would you have said? Would it have been honest?

2. How do you define real health now — as a woman, a mom, a human?

3. What have you unlearned about health that you want to pass on differently?

4. How do you encourage your daughter to listen to her *whole self*— not just her appearance or performance?

Journal Prompt

Write your own definition of health — not what culture says, but what you've learned it truly means. Then write a second version for your daughter.

Discussion Starters

These questions can help her begin exploring her own definition of real health.

- What do you think Luna realized about health while working on her project?

- Have you ever thought health was just about looks or weight? What do you think now?

- What are some signs that *you* feel healthy — not just physically, but mentally or emotionally?

- What does "real health" mean to you?

Tip: Avoid lecturing or over-correcting. Let her explore these ideas with curiosity—not pressure.

Creative Prompt or Activity

Invite your daughter to create her own "Real Health" reflection page.

She can begin with the prompt:

"Real health, to me, means…"

Encourage her to go beyond the physical and include things like:

- Being able to speak up when I need help

- Enjoying food without guilt

- Laughing and resting

- Moving because it feels good, not because I have to

- Feeling safe to be myself

You can create your own version alongside her.
Hang it somewhere visible, or tuck it away as a reminder on hard days.

Scripture Reflection

"Beloved, I pray that you may prosper in all things and be in health, just as your soul prospers." — 3 John 1:2

This verse connects physical wellness with soul wellness.

Talk about:

- What does it mean for your *soul* to be healthy?

- Do you think God cares about our minds and hearts as much as our bodies?

Let her know: God's vision for health is about *wholeness*, not appearance.

Closing Words for You

This chapter is about quiet bravery — the kind where a girl tells herself the truth and lets go of the performance.

If your daughter is learning to define health in her own words, she is already doing holy work.

Let her know she doesn't have to get it all figured out.
Let her know her journey is valid, even in progress.
Let her know that real health includes grace, joy, rest, and truth.

You're helping her find it—not through control, but through love.

9 THE WALL OF VOICES

Chapter Summary for Moms & Mentors

Luna finishes her "Real Health Project" — a collage full of truth, color, and heart —a nd pins it to the library bulletin board with a shaky hand. At first, she feels proud... but then the doubt creeps in.

What if it's too much? What if they think I'm weird? What if I regret this?

But then she sees it: a handwritten note from a classmate, tucked quietly next to her project.

"I thought I was the only one who had these thoughts. You were brave. Thank you."

Suddenly, Luna's voice becomes more than a project — it becomes a lifeline.
Her courage gave someone else permission to breathe, to be honest, to feel less alone.

And that's the heart of this chapter: we never know who is listening when we speak the truth.

Themes to Explore

- Vulnerability and second-guessing

- The ripple effect of honesty

- Fear of being seen — and the relief when we are

- Community born from courage

- Girls supporting girls in healing

Reflect & Connect

For you, Mama (or Mentor):

1. Have you ever shared something honest and immediately felt unsure — only to realize later that it helped someone else?

2. What stops you from sharing your story sometimes? Where do you still fear being "too much" or misunderstood?

3. How can you create a culture in your home (or classroom, or church) that honors honesty over perfection?

4. What are your own "voices" that still echo in your mind — whose approval or rejection are you afraid of?

Journal Prompt

Write about a moment when someone else's vulnerability gave you the courage to be honest. What did it unlock in you?

Discussion Starters

This chapter offers a tender chance to talk about courage, connection, and fear.

- Why do you think Luna started second-guessing her project after putting it up?

- Have you ever felt proud of something and then suddenly unsure or scared?

- What do you think that classmate's note meant to Luna?

- Do you believe that *your* honesty could help someone else feel less alone?

Tip: Remind her that bravery isn't the absence of fear — it's doing the right thing even when fear is loud.

Creative Prompt or Activity

Create a "Wall of Voices" together—either in her room, a shared notebook, or digitally.

Invite her to:

- Write down a truth she wishes someone had told her

- Add a quote or affirmation that reminds her she's not alone

- Include a story, poem, or reflection that represents her experience

You can contribute your own too.

Over time, this wall becomes a living reminder that her voice matters—and that other girls feel the same way she does.

Optional: Write a note to her (or have her write one to herself) that simply says: *"You are brave. Your honesty is helping someone else heal."*

Scripture Reflection

"Therefore encourage one another and build each other up." — 1 Thessalonians 5:11

Talk about:

- What does it mean to "build each other up" with our words or actions?

- Have you ever been encouraged by someone who didn't even know you needed it?

- How can *we* be encouragers, not just consumers of others' stories?

Remind her: her story is not a burden. It's a blessing in someone else's storm.

Closing Words for You

This chapter is a mirror — for your daughter, and maybe for you too. It asks: What if the thing you're most afraid to say is exactly what someone else needs to hear?

Let your girl know that her voice is holy. That when she speaks the truth about who she is and what she's walked through, she becomes a builder of bridges, not walls.

Your support, your listening, your affirmation — these are the scaffolding around her courage.

And never forget: your voice still matters too.

10 A LITTLE BIT BRAVE

Chapter Summary for Moms & Mentors

In this chapter, Luna stands in front of the school to present her Real Health Project. Her hands tremble. Her stomach turns. She wonders if she can really say it all out loud.

But then… she does.

She speaks from her heart — honestly, vulnerably, bravely — about what she's been through: the comment, the shame, the obsession, and the healing.

She expects silence. Maybe even judgment. But instead, the entire room rises to their feet. Applause. Tears. Connection.

A young teacher lingers after the presentation, deeply moved. She reflects on her own struggles at Luna's age and leaves her a quiet note: *"You were brave. You helped me heal too."*

This is the moment Luna realizes that bravery doesn't require being loud or perfect — it only requires being *willing*.

Themes to Explore

- Courage in the face of fear
- The healing power of truth-telling
- Generational impact of honesty
- How one voice can ripple outward
- Leading with vulnerability

Reflect & Connect

For you, Mama (or Mentor):

1. Can you recall a time when you were scared but did the brave thing anyway? What helped you push through the fear?

2. How do you model courage to your daughter — not the performative kind, but the kind that shows up when it matters?

3. What moments from your younger years still need healing? Could your daughter's journey be opening a door for you too?

4. How can you celebrate bravery in your daughter when it doesn't look "big" — when it's quiet, messy, and real?

Journal Prompt

Write about a time when someone else's story helped you heal something in yourself. What would you say to them if you could?

Discussion Starters

Invite reflection without pressure. Let her see that small bravery matters.

- What do you think helped Luna find the courage to speak in front of the school?

- Have you ever done something even though you were scared? What helped you do it?

- Why do you think the teacher was so moved by Luna's story?

- Do you believe your story could help someone else, even a grown-up?

Tip: Remind her that bravery isn't loud. It's choosing honesty even when your voice shakes.

Creative Prompt or Activity

Invite your daughter to write or draw about a moment when she was "a little bit brave." It doesn't have to be public or dramatic. It could be:

- Standing up for someone

- Saying how she really felt

- Asking for help

- Sharing her story

Then, invite her to write herself a short note of encouragement, starting with:

"Dear Me, I was brave when…"

You can write one too. Share them aloud or keep them as a reminder that courage comes in many forms.

Scripture Reflection

"Be strong and courageous. Do not be afraid; do not be discouraged, for the Lord your God will be with you wherever you go." — Joshua 1:9

Talk about:

- What does it mean to be courageous even when you're scared?

- How does it feel to know that God goes with us into the hard things?

- Is there something you want to do — but fear is holding you

back? Let her know: God doesn't just want her brave. He wants her whole.

Closing Words for You

There will be moments when your daughter steps into the spotlight of her own life — quivering, unsure, but willing. Those are holy moments. They shape her into the woman she is becoming.

Your job is not to remove the fear.
It's to remind her she can do hard things even *with* the fear.

Luna's journey shows us what happens when a girl tells the truth.
Other hearts begin to heal.
Old wounds begin to close.
And the world gets a little brighter, because one girl was brave enough to be seen.

You are raising that girl.

And you are becoming her, too.

11 THE KITCHEN LIGHT

Chapter Summary for Moms & Mentors

In this chapter, Luna finds herself in a quiet, intimate moment with her mom — under the soft glow of the kitchen light, long after the day has ended. It's in that stillness that her mom shares something she's never said out loud:

"You're the girl I always wanted to be."

She tells Luna how she grew up afraid to be herself. Afraid to take up space, to speak the truth, to love her body and trust her voice. Watching Luna grow, stumble, rise, and choose truth has been healing—for her too.

It's a sacred reminder that healing isn't just top-down. It moves in circles.
From mother to daughter.
From daughter to mother.
From woman to woman.

In this moment, they see each other fully. Not as roles—but as souls.

Themes to Explore

- Generational healing

- Mother-daughter connection

- Seeing your child as a mirror

- Vulnerability across age gaps

- Love as a bridge, not a finish line

Reflect & Connect

For you, Mama (or Mentor):

1. Has your daughter's journey ever awakened something in *you* that still needed healing?

2. Are there parts of yourself you buried as a girl to feel safe, accepted, or small enough to fit in?

3. What would your younger self say if she could sit in your kitchen today, watching your daughter grow?

4. Have you ever told your daughter that she inspires you—or are you afraid to say the quiet, sacred things?

Journal Prompt

Write a letter to your daughter that begins: *"Watching you has helped me..."* Or write a letter to your younger self, from the mother you are now.

Discussion Starters

Let this moment be soft. Tender. Shared without pressure.

- What did you think when Luna's mom said she was the girl she always wanted to be?

- Have you ever wondered if grown-ups still carry insecurities or fears?

- What do you think it means to *inspire* someone without even trying?

- How do you think moms and daughters help each other grow?

Tip: If this hits close to home, let your daughter see your heart. Tears are not a weakness — they're an invitation.

Creative Prompt or Activity

Invite your daughter to write a short note to herself in the mirror of time — either to her future self or younger self.

You can do the same.
Then swap notes — or read them aloud under the soft light of your own kitchen.

Optional prompts:

- "I want you to know you were always…"

- "What I see in you now is…"

- "Even when I didn't understand you, I always…"

This moment becomes a touchstone for your connection—and your shared healing.

Scripture Reflection

"He will turn the hearts of the parents to their children, and the hearts of the children to their parents." — Malachi 4:6

Talk about:

- What does it mean to really *see* your parent or your child?

- Have you ever felt like your heart softened toward someone in a moment of truth?

- How do love and honesty heal generations?

This verse is a quiet promise—that God weaves hearts together through truth and tenderness.

Closing Words for You

This chapter is a gift. It's a reminder that even when we're raising girls, we're still becoming women. That healing doesn't stop at adulthood. And that motherhood is not just guidance — it's transformation.

Let your daughter know that her light doesn't just shine forward — it shines backward, too.
Into your story. Into your wounds. Into the girl you once were, who still lives inside you.

Because sometimes the greatest healing comes not from being the teacher, but from becoming the student again.

And this… this is what legacy really looks like.

12 SPRINKLES AND SUNSHINE

Chapter Summary for Moms & Mentors

In this final chapter, Luna is no longer battling her body. She's not obsessed with shrinking it, fixing it, or comparing it. She's *enjoying* it. Laughing in it. Dancing, eating, resting, and connecting — with no apology.

She eats ice cream with sprinkles. She walks with sunshine on her skin. She notices beauty in others — not to compare, but to celebrate. She's present, awake, and filled with wonder.

This isn't the end of her story — but it *is* the moment she comes home to herself.

She now knows:
Her body is not broken.
Her worth is not up for debate.
And joy is not something she has to earn — it's something she's allowed to feel, every single day.

Themes to Explore

- Embodiment and joy

- Freedom from shame

- Appreciation for life, not performance

- Presence over perfection

- Coming home to yourself

Reflect & Connect

For you, Mama (or Mentor):

1. What does "coming home to yourself" mean to you? Have you experienced that yet?

2. Are you comfortable enjoying your body — not just tolerating it, but living in it fully and joyfully?

3. How do you express joy around food, movement, and life in front of your daughter?

4. What would it look like to give yourself permission to enjoy your life — with sprinkles and sunshine?

Journal Prompt

What part of your life or body have you been too serious about? Where can you invite joy, softness, or play back in?

Discussion Starters

Let this chapter feel like a celebration — not of "fixing," but of being.

- What do you think it means to come home to yourself?

- When do you feel most like *you*?

- What does joy feel like in your body?

- What would it look like to live every day with sprinkles and sunshine — even when it's cloudy?

Tip: Use this as a moment to anchor her in gratitude — not as a discipline, but as a gift.

Creative Prompt or Activity

Invite your daughter to create a *Joy Map* — a simple, colorful drawing or list of things, moments, people, and places that help her feel fully alive.

Encourage her to include:

- Things that make her laugh

- Foods she loves without guilt

- People who make her feel safe

- Activities that make her forget to check the mirror

- Places she feels free

You can do one too. Hang them up as reminders of what *home inside yourself* really feels like.

Scripture Reflection

"You will go out in joy and be led forth in peace; the mountains and hills will burst into song before you." — Isaiah 55:12

Talk about:

- What does it mean to be "led forth in peace"?

- Can joy and peace exist even after struggle?

- What would your life look like if joy was the guide instead of fear?

Let her know: this is God's desire — not just for obedience, but for *wholeness and delight.*

Closing Words for You

This chapter is a celebration.
A reminder that joy is not earned — it's received.
That you, too, are allowed sprinkles and sunshine, laughter and rest, wonder and play.

As Luna comes home to herself, may you come home, too.
May her freedom awaken your own, and may her light remind you of the girl you once were — the one who still lives inside you.

Because sometimes the greatest gift we give our daughters is showing them what it looks like to live fully, freely, and without apology.

AUTHOR'S NOTE

Mama, mentor, guide — *you did it.*

You showed up for this journey — not just to walk with her through Luna's story, but to walk *yourself* through it too.

Maybe you've remembered things you tucked away.
Maybe you've healed something that's been waiting.
Maybe you've written or even spoken words out loud you never knew how to say before.

Wherever this book has met you, I hope it reminded you of this:

You don't need to have it all together to be a powerful guide.

You just need to keep showing up. With gentleness. With truth. With love.

She is watching, observing. looking up to you. Not for perfection — but to light the way.

So laugh. Rest. Dance. Eat ice cream. Walk in the sunshine.

Because you're allowed to come home to yourself, too.

May she grow strong in truth, tender in spirit, and rooted in the light that never leaves her.

May *you* remember that it's never too late to heal.

And may your journey together be filled with sprinkles, sunshine, and the kind of love that changes generations.

With all my heart,

~Wendy 🤍

ABOUT THE AUTHOR

Wendy Leonard is a registered dietitian, entrepreneur, and mother of four who believes in the power of food, faith, and storytelling to transform lives. She's the author of *The Light Inside Luna* and the founder of Rhode Island Nutrition Therapy, where she helps individuals learn to love their bodies through nourishment, compassion, connection and truth.

Wendy wrote this companion guide for the women raising, mentoring, and loving girls in today's world because she knows firsthand how messy and difficult that journey can be — but that it can also be a place of healing.

Her work is rooted in a deep belief that when we speak honestly and love courageously, we don't just help the next generation heal — we heal ourselves in the process.

When she's not working with her team or hanging out with her husband or her kids, you can find her roaming a new country or sitting on her sofa with a cup of tea and a heart full of vision.

She hopes this book helps you come home to yourself, too.

Connect with Wendy at:
wendy@rinutritiontherapy.com

www.ingramcontent.com/pod-product-compliance
Lightning Source LLC
Chambersburg PA
CBHW031259120626
46545CB00007B/2896